Not since we last heard from Wormwood's uncle has an author so masterfully employed Lewis's *Screwtape* motif to simultaneously entertain, expose, convict and challenge the human heart. This book is a sanctified riot!"

Reggie Weems
Pastor and C.S. Lewis Scholar

If everything you say is always loving and life-giving then you can give this book a miss. But for the rest of us *The Scuttlebutt Letters* is a great resource. Drawing deeply on biblical wisdom, its intriguing and engaging presentation hits home time after time. It not only dissects the good and bad of our speech; it offers true hope.

Tim Chester
Senior Faculty, Crosslands Training

A modern allegory to deal with the age-old problem of keeping our lips under control, *The Scuttlebutt Letters* is clever, funny and a powerful reminder that, at heart, it is our hearts which need changing.

Ros Clarke
Associate Director, Church Society

The Scuttlebutt Letters is a must-read for every believer with a tongue. With honest insight, clever humour, and theological care, Natalie shows the trappings of sinful speech and the gospel remedy for self-deceived hearts. Her writing is a delight, and her message is timely.

Cheryl Marshall
Co-Author, *When Words Matter Most*

Natalie has written a rare jewel – something not only deliciously playful but also theologically rich and deeply convicting. With deftly crafted, witty prose, she ultimately leads our convicted hearts and tongues to the sweetest Word – Christ himself.

Felicity Carswell and Sarah Dargue
Two Sisters and a Cup of Tea podcast

Our day is marked by the misuse and careless use of words, in conversation with one another and especially online. In *The Scuttlebutt Letters*, Natalie Brand gives us a much-needed reminder of the power of the tongue through humor and wit. This short book will inspire you to examine your words and your heart in light of God's Word, while making you laugh along the way.

Walter Shaw
@WTSreads

Natalie Brand has written in a disarming style, and with frightening accuracy, of the way our tongues get out of control with gossip, exaggeration, lies, deflection, boasting, ridicule and more. I was not sure at times whether to laugh, wince or cry, but it is a healthy reflection leading to repentance, as we place our trust in the one who spoke with truth, wisdom and grace.

Graham Nicholls
Director of Affinity;
author, *Reasoning in the Public Square*

The Scuttlebutt Letters

Words to a Wild Tongue

Natalie Brand

CHRISTIAN
FOCUS

10 9 8 7 6 5 4 3 2 1
Copyright © Natalie Brand 2024
ISBN: 978-1-5271-1116-5
Ebook: 978-1-5271-1154-7

Published in 2024 by
Christian Focus Publications
Geanies House, Fearn, Tain, Ross-shire,
IV20 1TW, Scotland, U.K.
www.christianfocus.com
email: info@christianfocus.com

Cover design by
Pete Barnsley

Printed and bound by Gutenberg, Malta

CONTENTS

To those I have hurt with my words,
I am truly sorry.
NAMB

The heart is deceitful above all things,
and desperately sick;
who can understand it?
(Jer. 17:9)

Preface

The Screwtape Letters continues to transfix readers because Jack's imaginative dialogue, revealing the wily ways of demons and how they might manipulate the human heart, destabilises not only diabolical strategy in our lives (which we had not detected) but also our own fickle, fallen nature. Lewis creatively, and somewhat humiliatingly, persuades us that far too often our hearts (and minds) are ripe and ready for demonic manipulation.

Undermining the human heart has its successes. When we expose the heart for what it is, we are not so easily fooled by it. It is perhaps surprising then, in light of Jeremiah 17:9, that Christian satire remains an undeveloped genre. I believe ridiculing and mocking what is notoriously self-deceptive gets good results. Too long has the heart safely stewed in its own pride and self-righteousness. My dear reader, I am sure you know of what I speak. For have you not seen, when levelled with an attack or a challenge, how, with lightning speed, your heart turns the tables, passes the buck, cries 'foul play!', and justifies itself? Even licking its wounds in self-pity.

But this little book is not only about the heart but also the tongue. The Lord Jesus taught that our speech betrays what is hidden deep within. 'Out of the abundance of the heart the mouth speaks' (Matt. 12:34). If we want to gain godly control of our words, it is the heart that must change first. So, you see why in this project – birthed from a personal desperation for godly speech (*enough is enough*) – I have made full use of Holy God-breathed Scripture, as well as Jack Lewis's more subversive satirical method.

1. Delicious

The words of a whisperer are like delicious morsels.
(Prov. 18:8)

My Dear Scuttlebutt,

You must not be offended by my new nickname for
you. Whilst it is not very flattering, I have heard far
more obscene name-calling from you many times. It
came to mind after today's shameful incident with
the oily-faced gentleman at the office water-cooler.
Scuttlebutt is naval slang for the ship's gossip. On
the great galleons of old, a scuttled drum (that is,
a water barrel with a hole bored through it) was
always available on deck for the sailors to quench
their thirst. It was here that the seamen would
chinwag and curse about their superiors, blathering
out whatever was churning on the ship's rumour
mill. Obviously, not much has changed. Today's
events demonstrate that the congregation of workers
queuing for a drink is too convenient an opportunity
for idle tongues to wag.

I was horrified when that greasy man, whom
I like to call the OOT (Official Office Tattletale),

leant forward and whispered the latest dish towards our Left Ear. I saw you licking the Lips and your tastebuds were thrown into a level of delight normally reserved for scones and cream! Proving true the words from the Wisest of Books:

> The words of a whisperer are like delicious morsels;
> they go down into the inner parts of the body.
> (Prov. 18:8; 26:22)

I have yet to ask the Stomach if the seductive slander you so enjoyed has had any adverse effects to its lining. Surely you are sensible enough to know that while these scraps of gossip might taste sweet as they hit your apex, they soon turn sour and rancid, ruining our insides. It is curious that the extraordinary sensitivity of your palate (of which you have boasted many times) failed to taste the bitterness of the OOT's words.

What is most alarming, however, is that you then chose to correct the careless man's misinformation with what only smacked of further gossip. All whilst bathing in your own virtue. What did you enjoy more? Receiving those tasty titbits, or serving them out? BLABBERMOUTH! A more astute organ, like myself, would have made time to chew over the OOT's motive, taking note of his perfidious grin and gaudy tie. You really ought to consult me before you start contorting vowels and consonants. Otherwise,

I will speak to the Lungs and command them to deprive you of air. That would silence you!

Yes, *Scuttlebutt* suits you well. Now, I know you will defend yourself by placing the blame on me. Reminding me that I fluttered at the OOT's mouth-watering jawing. If I did, I was only pumping faster to meet the demands of your excitement. I have not your taste for other people's flaws or failings. And it certainly wasn't me who urged you to serve out further intelligence on the admitted incompetence of the office management. I suppose that was the work of the insipid cloud of Grey Matter up top.

All this said, my dear Scuttlebutt, you are not entirely guilty. You and I are only body organs. We cannot be held responsible for our human's bad decisions. He should certainly know better than to socialise 'with men of falsehood' and 'consort with hypocrites'.[1] It is these worthless gossipers who speak with crooked speech, devising evil behind our back.[2] Their every word is a covert assassin deployed to destroy the one of whom they speak. Was this not the case for King David? He knew the whisperers were his enemies, devising his downfall and destruction. 'All who hate me whisper together about me; they

---

1. Psalm 26:4.

2. Proverbs 6:12-14, 18.

imagine the worst for me.'[3] Were you not just like King David's conspirators today as you defamed our human's leaders? That tantalising tang of malicious whispers only comes from your desire to see the misfortune and ruin of others – a perverse appetite indeed! And both Ears joined in on your feast of fibs. It proves the inspired proverb, 'A liar gives ear to a mischievous tongue.'[4] As the book of Job says, 'Does not the ear test words as the palate tastes food?'[5] So you have more in common with the Ears than we knew. Perhaps this is why supermarkets sell those magazines full of juicy celebrity scandal right next to the snacks.

In all this, my dear Scuttlebutt, you need my wisdom and guidance. Through the forgotten art of letter-writing, I will self-sacrificially work for your improvement. For all our sakes! You might be unpredictable, but I am constant and reliable – a steady beating drum. And whatever you might have been told over the years, be assured, dear fellow, that my four chambers are full of affection for you.

Your Moral Metronome,

H

---

3. Psalm 41:5-7.

4. Proverbs 17:4.

5. Job 12:11.

P.S. There are some strategies useful for the alleviation of guilt in gossiping. One is particularly fitting for the Christian – a precious prelude you will have heard from numerous church women. First, you sigh deeply as though much burdened, frown with a little fervour and say in a careful tone, 'Now, I am telling you this for the sake of your prayers . . .' Then you are free to spout unfortunate news of all kinds, spreading 'secrets of which the knowledge proves the teller wise.'[6]

---

6. J. R. R. Tolkien, *The Silmarillion* (London: HarperCollins, 1999, first published George Allen 1977), 69.

2. Wild

No human being can tame the tongue.
(James 3:8)

My DEAR SCUTTLEBUTT,

It is apt that your nickname is of a nautical nature, for you are a tiny rudder directing this vast human ship, and you always steer us into catastrophe.[1] Small as you are, you possess considerable brawn. The Good Book has it, 'The tongue is a small member, yet it boasts of great things.'[2] It does not bode well to think of the destruction you would unleash if you were freed from this body. What a mercy then that you are tethered at the back, making escape from your cage-like cave impossible. It is astounding then (caged and shackled as you are) that you remain untameable.

> For every kind of beast and bird, of reptile and sea creature, can be tamed and has been tamed by mankind, but no human being can tame the tongue.
> (James 3:7-8)

---

1. James 3:4.
2. James 3:5.

You must be very strong indeed if mightier beasts, hundreds of times larger than you, have been domesticated (Siberian Huskies), destroyed to near extinction (Sumatran tigers), or wiped out completely (fire-breathing dragons). I suppose it is your constant exercise that keeps you so healthy and resilient, since you never rest, constantly prattling on, wittering away whether someone is listening or not. You are a 'restless evil'.[3] Even at night you mutter away quietly or cry out in the pained constraints of sleep.

What trouble you landed us all in today when that young and arrogant executive, the Artful Dodger, and his spineless sidekick the OOT, made those jeering comments during lunch hour. A little light laugh from you would have kept our human's popularity. But your pride was damaged because the OOT had turned against us after his confidence yesterday. Your outburst rendered us the fool. Remember, 'He who has a hasty temper exalts folly.'[4] And of course our enemies would employ the timeless excuse of 'only joking' or 'just a bit of banter'.[5] Now we are not only the fool but also the villain. BLOCKHEAD! You should have pre-empted their cunning. Perhaps this

---

3. James 3:8.

4. Proverbs 14:29.

5. Proverbs 26:18-19.

game of subtleties is too sophisticated for such a savage beast as yourself.

Yes, *beast* describes you well, for you exhibit ferocious speed. There is only One who can keep ahead of you, knowing what you are going to say before you say it.[6] Take this afternoon with the old dear in the Rover driving at snail's pace. In no time, you were sputtering fumes together with the exhaust. Spewing word-lava 'full of deadly poison'.[7] And how quickly your huffing and puffing turned into honking and hooting. I could barely distinguish between you and the horn!

You stain the rest of us decent and respectable members with your fierce words.[8] O untameable ~~fiend~~ friend (school-boy error), I am the seat of the human's honour and integrity, yet you ruin me. Alas, Sacred Writ assures us that not one of your tiny, speckled papillae can be reined in by our human.[9] The fact that you are wilder than all beasts, reptiles, and sea creatures, seems inconceivable when you remember the great and terrible Leviathan. What did they write of that legendary monster?

---

6. Psalm 139:4.

7. James 3:8.

8. James 3:6.

9. James 3:8.

Can you draw out Leviathan with a fishhook or press down his tongue with a cord? Can you put a rope in his nose or pierce his jaw with a hook? ... Will you play with him as with a bird, or will you put him on a leash for your girls? ... [None] can strip off his armour [or] come near him with a bridle.

(Job 41:1-2, 5, 13)

On earth there was not his like.[10] Yet we are told that this monster was tamed and destroyed, and you remain not so.[11] I believe the other organs have purchased for you some equestrian gear anyway. Of course, our human will not look as elegant as a horse donned with tack and harness. Indeed! You will look thoroughly ridiculous with a jointed snaffle in the Mouth and leather straps hanging from the Nose. But it is a delightful picture for me, since it will certainly incapacitate you for good!

Your Affectionate Fiend,

H

---

10. Job 41:33.
11. Psalm 74:13-14.

3. Fire

The tongue is a fire.
(James 3:6)

My Dear Scuttlebutt,

One of these days you are going to scuttle this human ship and cause us all to sink. Your behaviour today in the boardroom could have lost our human his career! When invited to give an update, you instantly played the part of *filibuster*, frantically pumping out a smoke screen of words to hide the truth of our human's procrastination. And when asked plainly if the project's deadline will be met, you carefully shifted the onus onto someone else, overstating the ineptitude of that rather green co-worker. Ah! The beauties of exaggeration; the lenient lie. Do you think mere embellishment of the truth will save you from the ugly brand of LIAR to your name? You fabricate by fiddling with the facts. Stretching out the truth so you can twist it more easily. In our human's mouth you coil, curl and conjure deceit like the Father of Lies making his first appearance in the garden.[1]

---

1. John 8:44; Genesis 3:1-7.

And you didn't leave it there. Afraid that you were as transparent as a jellyfish, you chose to win back favour by flattering the director. Under the warmth of your insincere gibberish, he melted into a puddle of overheated ego. FOOT-LICKER! Do you think your words honoured him? Flattery is only a lie thrown at another to place them in your debt – a malicious trap.[2] 'A lying tongue hates its victims, and a flattering mouth works ruin.'[3]

My dear Scuttlebutt, you think you have escaped trouble, but twice we are told 'a false witness will not go unpunished, and he who breathes out lies will not escape.'[4] Your little lies will spread into a wildfire. Irretrievable words move quicker than the wind. Remember the speed of school whispers hopscotching across the playground? *What is it about the human condition?* It seems there is something deep within humanity that is ripe for rumours. An inner kindling of crisp bone-dry leaves ready to be ignited, all too happy to fuel heat and hate towards others.[5] And the desolation can take years to undo.

---

2. 'A man who flatters his neighbour spreads a net for his feet' (Proverbs 29:5).

3. Proverbs 26:28. See Psalm 78:36.

4. Proverbs 19:5, 9.

5. Proverbs 26:21.

It is no surprise then that flames are described as *tongues* of fire. What destructive power there is in the flame of fibs. It reminds me of the infamous horror that unfolded at Pudding Lane. There, in a bakery belonging to Thomas Faryner on September 2nd in the year 1666, one tiny spark from an oven left medieval London in ashes. The diarist Samuel Pepys described it as 'a most horrid malicious bloody flame, not like the fine flame of an ordinary fire.'[6] Like the spread of lies, this flame mercilessly tore through London for four long days, licking up two-thirds of the city. It devoured:

> Eighty-nine churches, gates, the Guildhall, public edifices, hospitals, schools, libraries, a great number of blocks of buildings, 13,200 houses, 400 streets. Of the 26 wards of London, it utterly destroyed 15 and left 8 mutilated and half burnt.[7]

Over that week, Pepys watched his world succumb to the flames. 'With one's face in the wind you were almost burned with a shower of Firedrops … It made me weep to see it … all on fire and flaming at once, and a horrid noise the flames made, and the cracking

---

6. Samuel Pepys, *The Great Fire of London* (London: Penguin Classics, Penguin Random House, 2015), 34.

7. Inscription on the Monument (coordinates: Lat. 51.51021, Long. -0.08584) designed by Robert Hooke [1671-1677].

of houses at their ruine.'[8] One wonders how such a small fiery flake can ignite such devastation. Yet James likens you to this hellish heat:

> How great a forest is set ablaze by such a small fire! And the tongue is a fire, a world of unrighteousness. The tongue is set among our members, staining the whole body, setting on fire the entire course of life, and set on fire by hell.
>
> (James 3:5-6)

My dear Scuttlebutt, words create worlds. But your worlds are scorched, black and lifeless. You leave the living burnt and blistered. The preacher Spurgeon said, 'Tongue sins are great sins; like sparks of fire ill-words spread and do great damage.'[9] Still, my friend, humanity continues to deceive itself, excusing lies by dressing them in white. Can a lie be clothed in virtue? They are always red-hot, burning right through the very heart of God's law. The ninth commandment, 'You shall not lie' or 'bear false witness against your neighbour', is written in stone (literally). It was carved there by the very finger of God.[10] Forbidding 'anything

---

8. Pepys, Great Fire, 34.

9. C.H. Spurgeon, T*he Treasury of David: An Original Exposition of the Book of Psalms Vol. II* (London: Passmore and Alabaster, 1880), 238.

10. Exodus 20:16.

that undermines the truth.'[11] For when we lie, we forget God. We turn our backs on Him who is Truth personified and take on the very vernacular of Satan.

This was the case with Gehazi, the servant of the prophet Elisha. Gehazi burnt with lust for the gifts Elisha had refused from the cleansed Naaman. His greed for silver had him scurrying down the hill after the Syrian captain, telling him some taradiddle about two visitors newly arrived.[12] Gehazi weaved a tall tale: These guests were needy, the religious poor (sons of prophets), young, and feral (from the hill country). If anyone could benefit from Naaman's generosity, it would be them. Gehazi was cunning and asked only for a little of the abundance Naaman carried. He probably thought he was righting a wrong. After all, Naaman had been spared from leprosy and Elisha had rudely refused the gifts from an indebted pagan enemy.[13] Worst still was Gehazi's resolve to undermine Elisha and accept the gifts 'in the Lord's name' or 'by the life of Yahweh'. This blasphemy meant he broke the third commandment as well as the ninth.[14] Gehazi was obviously not that

---

11. Westminster Shorter Catechism 77, 78.

12. 2 Kings 5.

13. 2 Kings 5:20.

14. Dale Ralph Davies, *2 Kings: The Power and the Fury*, Focus on the Bible (Fearn, Ross-shire: Christian Focus, Repr. 2009), 97.

bright however, as he attempted to hide his actions from Elisha, a prophet who could hear what the King of Syria was speaking in his palace bedroom.[15] 'Where have you been Gehazi?' Elisha asked. And since Gehazi told Naaman a story, he has one for Elisha as well. One lie always leads to another. It was a whopper of just four words, "Your servant went nowhere."[16] The treachery is felt with Elisha's devastating words, "Did not my heart go when the man turned from his chariot to meet you?"[17] The parent cut by the lies of their child knows this well. "Was it a time to accept money and garments, olive orchards and vineyards, sheep and oxen, male servants and female servants?" Elisha asked him. Was God's salvation for sale? In his acceptance of Naaman's gifts, Gehazi cheapened grace. In his greed and lies, he forgot God. Blasphemy and deception worked hand in hand. And, as Proverbs tells us that the one with a dishonest tongue will fall into calamity, Naaman's leprosy clung to Gehazi.[18] And this was grace from the hand of God. Especially when we are reminded that God destroys the liar and

---

15. 2 Kings 6:11-12.

16. 2 Kings 5:25.

17. 2 Kings 5:26.

18. 2 Kings 5:27; Proverbs 17:20.

'abhors the bloodthirsty and deceitful man.'[19] What makes your distortion or exaggeration of the truth so removed from Gehazi's?

The Great Fire of London was only stopped in its tracks when houses and offices were sacrificed and pulled down. 'For lack of wood the fire goes out.'[20] I wonder whether this mysterious, highly flammable kindling within humankind also needs to be removed? In the meantime, I will dowse your conflagrations.

Your Cool Conscience,

H

---

19. Psalm 5:6.

20. Proverbs 26:20.

4. Fool

The mouths of fools pour out folly.
(Prov. 15:2)

My Dear Scuttlebutt,

What a good fellow you are to keep me so entertained. Encased as I am, with such an interior anatomical position, I do miss out on a good joke. But I have not stopped snickering since the party our human attended last night. Believe me, it was not your desperate gags that made me chortle.

I was aware of all your good intentions while our human sat in the taxi. You even had me persuaded that you were going to apply my instruction and hush up for once. If you did lose your resolve, I was confident the canapés would keep you occupied. But alas, you lasted only eleven minutes. Or did you confuse silence with holding your breath?

I watched the whole thing. After our human was welcomed, the growing presence of more people made you feel inferior and sidelined. Being ignored for five long minutes whilst standing by the drinks was an eternity for your pride. In hot shame, the Cheeks pinkened, the Eyes fell, and the Nerves frayed like an old rope. You couldn't help yourself. You needed to reassert yourself and the fastest way to do that was to poke fun at the other guests. Whilst your hearers might have only heard humorous wisecracks regarding the dress and facial hair of those women in the room unfamiliar to you, your words were laced with hate and contempt. SCUTTLEBUTT! You certainly lived up to your nickname. Are you really so insecure that you need to attack the unknown friends of your host? Whilst your witty quips and quibbles may have won respect with the unrespectable, you lost credibility with the credible. It amazes me that you are so desperate to emit noise you are happy with drivel and twaddle as long as it produces laughter. O, what a spectacular fail! You see, my dear Scuttlebutt, YOU were the joke I so enjoyed last night.

I do pity you, friend. Besides your role as food and wine taster, unless you speak, your existence is utterly pointless. But be warned! Since the party your popularity with the other organs and members has seriously diminished. Remember the ruination of Fyodor Pavlovich. He proved true the Wise King's promise that 'a babbling fool will come to ruin'.[1] And 'whoever guards his mouth preserves his life;

---

1. Proverbs 10:8-10.

[but] he who opens wide his lips comes to ruin'.[2] In *The Brothers Karamazov*, the babbler Pavlovich is so hated for his verbal diarrhoea. And he certainly met a dire end. He once blurted to a monk (with his verbal incontinence and false modesty he was in perpetual confession),

> 'I sometimes tell lies inappropriately, I do it even on purpose, on purpose to be pleasant and make people laugh … And that's how I am, it's always like that with me. I am forever damaging myself with my own courtesy.'[3]

Pavlovich knew he was thought a buffoon and so played the buffoon to endear himself to others. What weakness of mind! Perhaps you are not so different. You don't even have his good sense as to know why you jest and josh for attention. 'I'm a buffoon out of shame,' he said. 'I act up just because I am insecure.'[4] If only Pavlovich had learnt it is better to remain silent and be thought a fool than to speak out and remove all doubt. 'Even a fool who keeps silent is considered wise; when he closes his lips, he is deemed intelligent.'[5] It is interesting that the inventor of this

---

2. Proverbs 13:3.

3. Fyodor Dostoevsky, *The Brothers Karamazov* (London: Everyman's Library, 1997), 40-41.

4. Ibid, 43.

5. Proverbs 17:28.

character, Fyodor Dostoevsky, gave his foolish villain his own name. Was this false modesty or was he marking the truth that writers of books can be those chiefly guilty of speech-folly?

I am not saying all clowning around ends in death at the hand of one's children, as was the case with Pavlovich. But there is good reason why many of the barbaric punishments and tortures long outlawed in civilised society involved the tongue. Be assured, I am not threatening you, only stating a fact.

Yes, words are a hotbed for sin. Which is most disturbing because your average counterpart speaks between 10,000 and 20,000 words a day.[6] That is verbal carpet bombing! It is no surprise then, 'when words are many, transgression is not lacking.'[7] One expert says, 'We're simply too busy talking to stop and examine how we are doing it. After all, we don't want to interrupt ourselves!'[8] It is a matter of basic logic. If you open your mouth for too long, expelling a barrage of words like a blunderbuss, at least some will betray your position, your real nature. Whilst others, by force of fire, will embed themselves into the flesh of innocent bystanders.

---

6. Jeff Robinson, *Taming the Tongue: How the Gospel Transforms Our Talk* (The Gospel Coalition, 2021), 4.

7. Proverbs 10:19.

8. Robinson, Tongue, 36.

I have observed that there are times your speech even agitates you to further sin. For example, when you indulge in a rant regarding a wrong someone has committed, your words actually stir up more resentment than you felt to begin with. You preach to yourself a toxic sermon and listen to every word! Similarly, when you allow yourself a verbal vent, you are blithely unaware that you spray your hearers with your own self-absorption. Not only displaying your vanity but cultivating it. Thus, you multiply your crimes, whereas silence would confine them. Only 'a fool multiplies words.'[9] I have observed these things because I taste tinges of your injured pride from down here. But *only tinges!* DO NOT EMBROIL ME IN YOUR INSUFFERABLE DEPRAVITY!

[Here, the letter breaks off and then resumes in a neater hand.]

Apologies, my friend. In the heat of composition several of my blood vessels burst. But do not be alarmed; I am now resting and in a calmer state.

Dearest Scuttlebutt, I have noticed you willingly suffer in silence when a compliment is due. In these moments, you are as tight-lipped as ever. And you excuse your silence for shyness. Indeed, the self-

---

9. Ecclesiastes 10:14.

forgetfulness required in authoring a well-earned compliment would embarrass your pride considerably! In the rare times you do offer encouragement, you find it so excruciating it comes out only as a mumble or mutter.

King David – like Pavlovich – also suffered under the threat of patricide. But contrary to the unfortunate Pavlovich, this threat was not realised. Could this be because the wise King determined, 'I will guard my mouth with a muzzle'?[10] My dear Jibber-Jabber, if only I could walk our human down to the pet shop and purchase a muzzle myself. I would save the world from your waffle and flimflam.

Your Sagacious Friend,
H

P.S. Since writing the above I have been informed that due to your inability to curb yourself, the other members and organs have taken matters into their own hands and a formal complaint has been made to internal affairs.

---

10. Psalm 39:1.

5. Poison

The tongue is full of deadly poison.
(James 3:8)

MY DEAR SCUTTLEBUTT,

You are always on your best behaviour at church (at least in appearance). We shall use this to our advantage in winning you back some kudos with the other members. So continue in your habit of making your public prayers particularly loquacious. Though I have always found them nauseatingly rehearsed and repetitive, I will stomach them for the sake of your reparation. I recommend using those undignified words Christians associate with abject humility. For instance, calling yourself 'a vile worm' will have a most pleasing effect on the hearers. But show care! Maintain some decorum. Do not allow your listeners to actually think you are a worm, or that you are utterly undeserving like them. Do not debase yourself like those other church members I have seen shamefully beating their breasts like the pitiful tax collector.[1]

---

1. Luke 18:9-14.

I am sure we need not be overly concerned. Our human is a decent, upright sort of fellow, a respected member of the church. We can be certain he is held in high regard because he has never been asked to do any of the lowly maintenance work or cleaning. No doubt this is because everyone knows how extraordinarily generous he is in his tithe.

There was a time, many years ago, when our human did try to help with the washing-up. Upon entry to the kitchen, he was bustled away by a human *Dracaena trifasciata*. This keeper-of-the-kitchen epitomised why the snake plant, with its razor-sharp leaves laced with poisonous toxins, has also been caricatured Mother-in-Law's Tongue. This *objurgatrix*[2] banned our human from the kitchen and he has never returned. But not just mothers-in-law and church kitchen scolds, my serpentine Scuttlebutt! Humanity has been too quick to satirise these personalities, when in fact every human tongue (but one) has struck out with sharp words laced with venom. Words that sting the victim and make their hearts stop in agony, humiliation and despair. I write from experience. And paradoxically, it is always those

---

2. It is vexing that the author of these letters likes to use archaic words. No doubt so readers will think him clever. Because of this, a glossary of terms can be found in the appendices. Signed, *The Appendix*.

closest and most dear to the person speaking who suffer in this way.

The trouble with poison is it is unseen. It lurks secretly within. Indeed, it is this invisibility that makes it the choice tool of assassins. On the surface, everything looks harmless. You only know poison is present when it is too late, the sting has stung, the fangs have sunk into your flesh, the wound has turned septic and green. This is why the Lord called the Pharisees a brood of vipers. They were sterile on the outside but inside was death.[3] The Lord demanded of them, 'How can you speak good, when you are evil?'[4] Like you, they were double-tongued.[5] How can the same mouth speak love and hate, blessing and cursing at the same time?[6] It's almost polyphonic!

> No human being can tame the tongue. It is a restless evil. Full of deadly poison. With it we bless our Lord and Father, and with it we curse people who are made in the likeness of God.
>
> (James 3:8-9)

This is most apparent on Sundays. One moment you are singing out sacred words of praise to God and mere moments later you are slurring or snubbing

---

3. Matthew 23:27.

4. Matthew 12:34.

5. 1 Timothy 3:8.

6. James 3:10.

another member of the Body for some offence or inconvenience. O, it is rarely slander! You are too respectable for that. It is *slighting* – which might be a human rewording to minimise the same thing. Only slightly slander. How can one worship God from the same pew from which they judge their brothers and sisters in Christ? Let alone declare holy, eternal utterances from the same mouth with which they criticise. 'If anyone says, "I love God," and hates his brother, he is a liar.'[7] Are you even aware of your unjust spite towards the brother or sister beside you? Let alone the fact it taints your worship?

We need not wonder why James writes so much about the destructive power of the tongue in his sacred letter to the church. Obviously, he was watching this tiny muscle breaking up the Body. I know how he feels.

> What causes quarrels and what causes fights among you? Is it not this, that your passions are at war within you? You desire and do not have, so you murder. You covet and cannot obtain, so you fight and quarrel … Do not speak evil against one another, brothers. The one who speaks against a brother or judges his brother, speaks evil against the law and judges the law.
>
> (James 4:1-2, 11)

---

7. 1 John 4:20.

It is not only James who corrects as I do. There was poison on the island of Crete also. Paul wrote to these infamous liars and slanderers, 'Speak evil of no one, to avoid quarrelling, to be gentle, and to show perfect courtesy toward all people.'[8] Come to think of it, poisonous speech must have been a church-wide contaminate as many of the New Testament letters instruct the Christians to curb their tongues.[9] It seems there was no speech sin of which the early church were innocent. This problem was not restricted to Jeremiah's dark days when deceit was ever on the lips of the people. Brothers and sisters had learnt to 'bend their tongue like a bow' against one another.[10] The prophet writes, 'Every brother is a deceiver, and every neighbour goes about as a slanderer.'[11] Many were like the wicked who taste evil and find it sweet in their mouths, hiding it under their tongues, like the venom of cobras.[12] This evil was symptomatic of a deeper rebellion, a deeper hatred – one towards God.

---

8. Titus 3:2. See 1:12.

9. 1 Corinthians 14:1-39; Ephesians 4:15,25-26,29-31; Philippians 2:14; Colossians 4:6; 1 Thessalonians 2:4-5; 1 Timothy 3:11, 5:14; 2 Timothy 2:14, 16-17, 3:3; Titus 1:10-11, 2:3, 2:9, 3:2; 1 Peter 2:1, 3:10, 4:11; 2 Peter 2:18; 1 John 4:20.

10. Jeremiah 9:3.

11. Jeremiah 9:4.

12. Job 20:12-14.

Consequentially, judgement ensued, and Assyria laid the land bare.

> Therefore thus says the LORD of hosts: 'Behold, I will refine them and test them, for what else can I do, because of my people? Their tongue is a deadly arrow; it speaks deceitfully; with his mouth each speaks peace to his neighbour, but in his heart he plans an ambush for him.'
>
> (Jer. 9:7-8)

I suppose our speech is the real indicator of our spiritual maturity. What does that say about you? Are you a tongue that always speaks peace to your neighbour? I have noticed that in church relationships you are particularly loath to give the benefit of the doubt, whilst in the office you are reasonable, always reading arguments in context. At church you are quick to put 'the worst possible construct on other's motives, and when there is a less flattering interpretation you always go for that one.'[13] Is it news to you that pettifogging is not a spiritual discipline? And I haven't even mentioned your insincere small talk; robbing the freshly taught Word from the minds and hearts of your fellow members as you scratch around for conversation about the weather. And who is responsible for our human's

---

13. Kevin DeYoung, '12 Marks of a Quarrelsome Talker' (Appendix 2) in Robinson, *Tongue*, 26. [Italics given].

habit of using the direction of the pews to make a beeline for the important people, avoiding those he thinks to be unimportant, tedious or smelly? I shall speak to the Feet!

I suppose the venom you spit is from another source, one that escapes me completely. Perhaps our human is host to a poisonous parasite, and we've never known it?

It is fortunate that you have me, dearest Scuttlebutt. I am your anchor, your source, your epicentre. I believe there is something in the Good Book about you being the outlet, the aperture of my bubbling virtues?[14] I can only surmise that there is a blockage at your end.

Your Antidote,
H

P.S. The slighting of church siblings deserves a different tack if we are talking of the church leadership. Especially the pastor, after all, he is on the church payroll. Of course, I am not condoning those who entertain themselves on the drive home by tearing the sermon apart, nor those who, as they tuck into their roast dinner, slice up the pastor together with the meat and potatoes.

---

14. Matthew 15:18.

6. Knife

Rash words are like sword thrusts.
(Prov. 12:18)

My Dear Blind-Shanker,

I am told by some of the other members that you have informed them of my letters and found yourself incredibly witty in suggesting my signature of 'H' stands for hypocrite. I could call you a BACKSTABBING SWINE! But I am only grieved that in all my care and concern for you, you can only lash out with insults.

Your betrayal reminds me of a harrowing confrontation our human had with his parents years ago. Your cruel words still haunt me. Only you could escalate a conversation of filial warmth into a sparring match before the froth on the coffees had diminished.

I remember it well. First, you started to nag the poor old couple. This is a torture you alone can administer, tormenting the victim with your racket until they succumb. The unfortunate Samson was punished in this way by not one female but two.

His first wife (a marriage that didn't outlive its celebrations) wept and nagged the strong man to tell his playful riddle for seven long days. Even this man of unrivalled brawn weakened under the torment of the tongue.[1] And Delilah did similarly for another riddle, the riddle of Samson's strength.

> And she said to him, 'how can you say, "I love you," when your heart is not with me? You have mocked me these three times, and you have not told me where your great strength lies.' And after she pressed him hard with her words day after day, and urged him, his soul was vexed to death. And he told her all his heart.
> (Judg. 16:15-17)

I am sure you left the old folk in a similar state as Delilah left Samson, beaten and betrayed. And just as the defeated Samson told this feminine Judas, bought with 1,100 pieces of silver, 'all his heart', so you spouted secrets of mine that were not yours to tell. You treacherous TATTLETALE! But you had only just begun. Like a sword you were merely sharpening yourself on a whetting stone, readying yourself for an ambush.[2] You could at least be a gentleman and give your victims warning.

En garde!

---

1. Judges 14:16-17.

2. Psalm 64:3-4.

Fired by frustration and anger because your expectations were not met, you then lost your temper. You slashed and gashed with sword thrusts those who bounced us lovingly on their knee.[3] If anyone should be saved from your onslaught, surely it is these good people? Doesn't this violence make us the old folks' enemy? King David characterises those bloodthirsty dogs sent to kill him in this very way. 'There they are, bellowing with their mouths *with swords in their lips.*'[4]

The shame of hearing the ugliness of your words made you even more angry. Like the fool, you gave 'full vent' to your spirit.[5] In fact, Scripture tells us the fool is better off, 'Do you see a man who is hasty in his words? There is more hope for a fool than for him.'[6] All this was then inflamed by the sobs of our human's mother. And when our father rebuked you for your careless words, you only made a wordless scoff – a truly grotesque sound. It was a perfect play-act of the proverb, 'A wise son hears his father's instruction, but a scoffer does not listen to rebuke.'[7] Now we are a scoffer as well as a fool! One of those

---

3. Proverbs 12:18.

4. Psalm 59:6-7.

5. Proverbs 29:11.

6. Proverbs 29:20.

7. Proverbs 13:1.

who curse 'their fathers and do not bless their mothers … Whose teeth are swords, whose fangs are knives.'[8]

Unkind words can scar forever. They maim the self-esteem and lacerate relationships. You only won the spar because the old folks were not prepared to cut you as deep as you cut them. Their love gave you opportunity for victory and you knew it.

One writer, a rarity-of-a-man who authored a leading history on the inhumanity of humanity, describes well the brutality of the tongue:

> She managed everything with just her sharp agile tongue. She didn't lift a finger. But it seemed as if she were invisibly whipping him across the cheeks, because spots, spots of red, flamed on his lusterless womanlike skin, and his ears blushed crimson and his lips twitched.[9]

Her victim had only called her out for being late.

Touché!

Will our parents ever forget your cruel words? Can you? The hurtful words echoing in our heads rarely lose volume. Like swords, words cut right to the heart. I know this because I have felt it. I am

---

8. Proverbs 30:11,14.

9. Aleksandr I. Solzhenitsyn, *The Gulag Archipelago 1918-1956: An Experiment in Literary Investigation Vol.2* (New York: HarperPerennial, 2007), 274-275.

always with you as you deliver your stinging blows. And if your words wound the heart within you, imagine what they are doing to your victim! I still bear scars from that hard-nosed teacher and that bitter aunt.

Of course, it is not always what you say but how you say it. Unfortunately, when it comes to non-musical tone, no one is tone deaf. And tone is especially volatile when humans live together, within the family. It is telling that in a rather ominous correspondence between two demons – that I was once privy to – the senior tempter stressed the diabolical use of tone to his nephew and protégé.

> In civilised life domestic hatred usually expresses itself by saying things which would appear quite harmless on paper (the words are not offensive) but in such a voice, or at such a moment, that they are not far short of a blow in the face.[10]

This tempter seeks 'the delightful situation of a human saying things with the express purpose of offending and yet having a grievance when offence is taken.'[11] Such duplicity in speech cannot be ignored or excused if a veteran tempter from the underworld sees it as useful for growth in self-idolatry and

---

10. C. S. Lewis, *The Screwtape Letters* (Woking: Unwin Brothers, 1942), 22-23.

11. Ibid, 23.

destructive in family relationships. So, passion or colour in your tone or pitch have behind them something more sinister than the mere demands of family life.

Not all such tactics are to be written off, however. There are harmless manoeuvres that allow one to remain blameless in a disagreement, giving the ability to say what you want without actually saying it. The first is done at the moment of retort. First, start your sentence and say enough of it to make your meaning clear. But then drop off and add 'it doesn't matter' while meekly shaking the Head. The timing is delicate, but if employed well it can be most effective. Thus, you can say almost anything but are not culpable because you decided not to say it. Some may confuse this with manipulation or a buttery forked tongue, as in the proverb, 'His speech was smooth as butter, yet war was in his heart; his words were softer than oil, yet they were drawn swords.'[12] But I am sure such passive-aggression would not be found in my repertoire!

There is also the extreme version of this, commonly known as the silent treatment. This method demonstrates that silence isn't always the fruit of grace or self-control. Here you don't even need to start an unfinished sentence but can use

---

12. Psalm 55:21.

angry withdrawal as a weapon against those who have wronged you. (The facial muscles really come into their own.) This silent assault gives you the freedom to fume without saying anything. In my observation this strategy suits personalities who do not find it tasteful to bellow but want to be angry all the same.

Yours Regretfully,
H

P.S. I have received a formal letter from internal affairs, formally known as L.O.P.I.T.O.F.F (The Limbs, Organs, and Parts Investigative Taskforce for the Ousting of the Factious and inFected [I guess they realised this acronym didn't really work]). It seems I am under investigation. What a nerve these bureaucrats have! Why should I – of all organs – be a suspect? What have you said to them?

P.P.S. In hindsight, perhaps I have been too hard on you. Believe me, your best interests are always at heart. Still, I will address you in a softer tone.

7. Boast

The tongue makes great boasts.
(Ps. 12:3)

My Sweet Child,

My ventricles are still drumming with the Artful Dodger's inane gassing today. That braggart makes egotism an artform! I suppose he has never heard the Proverb, 'Let another praise you, and not your own mouth; a stranger, and not your own lips.'[1] He boasts in whatever he finds opportunity: his golf swing, his sports car, his stubble, even his laziness, as he expertly ducks and darts away from all exertion and responsibility. His tongue wags and brags and there is nothing in the man but hot air!

Indeed, his boasting is quite a thing to watch. I observed in today's coffee break, as our human listened in utter boredom, that with every self-congratulating blast from his mouth this pretentious *popinjay* inflated. With each boast he swelled. Larger and rounder he grew. Yet from the inside. I do not know how. The mechanics of this elude me since I am

---

1. Proverbs 27:2.

the only one with interior valves. As he inflated, our human shrank. The agitated listener always shrivels up under the monstrous ego of a braggart. You had clearly had enough. So, as soon as he allowed himself to draw breath, you jumped in. Though you know the fellow to be ridiculous, you had to join him. Every boaster invites another. But because his self-worship is too blatant for you, his crows too crude, you went for the Christian alternative – the humblebrag. A brag 'in the guise of humility, putting a thin veneer of humble over a clear expression of proud.'[2] My dear Braggadocio, you did it well. I have found Christians are particularly gifted at articulating humblebrags.

> Feeling so blessed in the wonders and beauty of God's creation. *#whitesands #grandcayman*

Some can even put a self-righteous spin on them as well, especially those in ministry.

> One ministry after another – youth camps, beach missions, conferences all over the country, speaking engagements abroad. I'd really like some time at home for a change.

---

2. Tim Challies, 'The Art and Science of the Humblebrag.' (Accessed online 15/08/2023.) https://www.challies.com/articles/the-art-and-science-of-the-humblebrag/ [Emphasis mine].

Obviously the humblebrag is not in the Artful Dodger's dictionary; he didn't know what to make of it. No matter. In time you were both playing the same game. You were two oversized balloons nudging and bumping each other in turn, trying to outdo each other. But the way of the overinflated is inevitable … 'Clouds and wind without rain is a man who boasts of a gift he does not give.'[3] Empty words. Empty promises. BANG!! It was nothing but bluster. Guff. Effluvia.

Rehoboam was just the same: young and garrulous. He and his cocky cronies – the young men with whom he had grown up – thought themselves so witty. After his father King Solomon had died, the people of the northern realm came to the south and spoke to Rehoboam. 'Your father made our yoke heavy. Now therefore lighten the hard service of your father and his heavy yoke upon us, and we will serve you.'[4] There had been political unrest amongst the northern tribes of Israel, and this was Rehoboam's chance for a diplomatic solution. Indeed, the advisors of the late king gave the new king counsel to this end. 'Speak good words to them when you answer them, then they will be your servants forever.'[5] In short,

---

3. Proverbs 25:14.

4. 1 Kings 12:4.

5. Verse 7.

soft words will ensure the people's allegiance. 'A soft tongue will break a bone.'[6] The right word fitly spoken at this time would have been 'like apples of gold in a setting of silver.'[7] But Rehoboam's crown had gone to his head (figuratively). His power-hungry friends gave different advice. They trusted upon the resourcefulness of their own speech, like that prattling self-admiring peacock in the office. They were 'those who say, "With our tongue we will prevail, our lips are with us; who is master over us?"'[8] Rehoboam's chums fed his vanity and desire to assert his new royal prerogative. With language typical of young men, they coined a rather vulgar slogan to use that would attest to Rehoboam's virility.[9] One that ridiculed his father by boasts of greater physical manhood.

> And the young men who had grown up with him said to him, "Thus shall you speak to this people who said to you, 'Your father made our yoke heavy, but you lighten it for us,' thus shall you say to them, 'My little finger is thicker than my father's thighs. And now, whereas my father laid on you a heavy yoke, I will add to your yoke. My father

---

6. Proverbs 25:15.

7. Proverbs 25:11.

8. Psalm 12:4.

9. Bob Fyall, *Teaching 1 Kings: From Text to Message* Proclamation Trust (Fearn, Ross-shire: Christian Focus, 2015), 179.

disciplined you with whips, but I will discipline you with scorpions.'"

(1 Kings 12:10-11)

Rehoboam lapped it up, 'The king answered the people harshly, and forsaking the counsel that the old men had given him, he spoke to them according to the counsel of the young men.'[10] In Rehoboam's eyes there was only one king on the throne of Israel, and he was that king. He did not need to pander to the people and their inconsequential requests. So he stood before them and boasted in himself: his kingship, his manhood, his strength, his power, his domination. Here, Rehoboam did not just mock his father but chose to be the very antithesis of him. He rejected the call to 'get wisdom'[11] and so opposed all that his father, the Wise King, crafted in the book of Holy Riddles. How devastating when you see how much of it is a loving father's instruction to his beloved son. Rehoboam accepted the folly of his friends and delivered it persuasively. But 'Fine speech is not becoming to a fool; still less is false speech to a prince.'[12] His brash, beef-witted, foul-mouthed boast ended in only failure and ruin. 'When all Israel saw that the king did not listen to them, the people

---

10. 1 Kings 12:13-14.

11. Proverbs 4:5-9.

12. Proverbs 17:7.

answered the king, "What portion do we have in David? We have no inheritance in the son of Jesse. To your tents, O Israel! Look now to your own house, David.'"[13] So Israel rebelled and separated from Judah, never to return. His mindless boasting damaged and split the kingdom in half! A move that destabilised the nation and would lead to the scattering of the twelve tribes. Certainly, the LORD was fulfilling His purpose.[14] But the story demonstrates that while boasting may be nothing but hot air, the fruit of it can be catastrophic. Rehoboam trusted in himself. He trusted in his boasts. And his kingdom crumbled.

Self-idolatry is the wind that gives voice to the braggart. Self-aggrandizement is only ever the futile hobby of fallen humanity. But there is one justified boast for the tongue:

> Let not the wise man boast in his wisdom, let not the mighty man boast in his might, let not the rich man boast in his riches, but let him who boasts boast in this, that he understands and knows me, that I am the LORD who practises steadfast love, justice, and righteousness in the earth. For in these things I delight, declares the LORD.
>
> (Jer. 9:23-24)

---

13. 1 Kings 12:16.

14. See verse 15.

I am told such is the only boast for the Christian, like that gospel loudmouth – the Apostle Paul. What did he say? 'Far be it from me to boast except in the cross of our Lord Jesus Christ, by which the world has been crucified to me, and I to the world.'[15] You, however, are nothing but a windbag.

Your Humble Friend,
H

---

15. Galatians 6:14.

8. Grave

Their throat is an open grave.
(Rom. 3:13)

My Dear Scuttlebutt,

Today I am befuddled. Last night, when our human decided to take the plunge and enter the world of social media, I was sure that I would finally enjoy some peace from your monotonous drone. However, the world our human tapped into was no different from our everyday physical world. There I was thinking I'd be safe from your fire and poison and it was all there! Typed into little boxes and threads of digital speech. Our human signed up for it all. Endless yarns of text – bickering and backbiting for one's leisure.

This world wasn't all antagonistic, there were reams of junk too: Fake news, click-baits for humanity's perverted appetite, and the narcissistic taking far too much pleasure in themselves. There were trolls there too. These trolls do not patrol bridges as commonly believed, but trawl through this digital speech, ready to catch people in nets. They ambush the innocent, making haste to shed virtual blood.[1] Jumping upon the words of others in a most unforgiving manner. Twisting and misrepresenting with a fury they would never express in person. This is especially true if the victim is someone of note. Then they discredit and defame. Even church leaders are attacked by disparaging comments, character assassinations, and theological misrepresentation. These trolls 'lie in wait for their own blood; [setting] … an ambush for their own lives.'[2] In seeking to catch others, they only ensnare themselves. For this realm is an invisible archive and every word is irretractable. Rash words in this space-without-walls bring public humiliation.

It was also a haven for fools. It seemed to give them a new freedom. I saw them strutting from app to app, platform to platform, with a sort of desperate self-love. It was a palace for Lady Folly, who we find in the Wisest of books. In truth she is no lady! She is loud, full of words without knowledge, and empty promises.[3] She calls the senseless to herself and the senseless indulge, hooked by her addictive pleasures. This screen-sized world epitomised her. Millions daily enter this sticky world wide web, even though they know it saps and drains their mental

1. Proverbs 1:10-11.

2. Proverbs 1:17-18.

3. Proverbs 9:13-17.

strength. They quite literally have 'their fill of their own devices'[4] but cannot remove themselves. Like the crew of Odysseus entrapped by the lotus-eaters. It is nothing short of a modern-day Circe's Island or Vanity Fair. In this unsociable media, the narcotic is collecting hollow approval, 'likes' and followers. In truth it is a Nothing, but

> Nothing is very strong: strong enough to steal away a man's best years not in sweet sins but in a dreary flickering of the mind over it knows not what and knows not why, in the gratification of curiosity so feeble that the mind is only half aware of them in drumming of fingers.[5]

As is the case with the guests of Lady Folly, these enticements only lead to the grave. 'As a bird rushes into a snare; he does not know that it will cost him his life.'[6]

It proves that we are snared by our words, digital or not.[7] They are chains upon us, iron cables that shackle the speaker. This is why the Great Book warns us about the uttering of vows or oaths. Words bind us:[8]

---

4. Proverbs 1:31.

5. Lewis, *Screwtape*, 64.

6. Proverbs 7:23.

7. Proverbs 6:2.

8. Numbers 30:6-16. See also Zechariah 8:16-17.

> If a man vows a vow to the LORD, or swears an oath
> to bind himself by a pledge, he shall not break his
> word. He shall do according to all that proceeds out
> of his mouth.

> (Num. 30:2)

Because words are never *just* words. Words make
worlds. Indeed, our universe began with words.
In the beginning, the Creator spoke and called
everything from nothing. God gave humanity, 'made
in his image', His own ability to communicate.[9] In
doing this He gave more than a bodily faculty;
He shared His own communicative nature.[10] This
means that at the heart of humans imaging their
Creator – reflecting his nature, displaying His
excellencies – are the words you shape and sound!
More than this; speech as God's image-bearers is
the imitation of the very triunity of God. For the
Triune God is the Father – the Speaker, the Son
– the Word, and the Spirit – the Breath. Yet your
disregard of what comes out of your mouth profanes
this profound privilege.

Because with words you *act*. Words carry out an
action. You request, warn, invite, promise, apologise,
predict or resign. You 'make something the case by

---

9. Genesis 1:26-27.

10. Robinson, *Tongue*, 8-9.

saying that it is.'[11] You birth a promise when you say, 'I promise to empty the bins.' When you say, 'I resign', you have *resigned*. It is an action by speech, a speech act. And any intention contrary to your words is an abuse of speech and integrity. In certain situations, and offices, one doesn't even need to voice the speech act but can just say, 'You are husband and wife' and it is so. So too in naming a great ship, announcing guilt in a court of law, or declaring a country to be at war. Words are never empty. They make. They undo. They form covenants and they break them. 'Death and life are in the power of the tongue.'[12] Yes, my lackadaisical friend, your words direct this very life. They can form a sweet, lifelong, legally binding covenant before God on a wedding day. But words of death can threaten divorce in the heat of an argument. And deadly are the words – smooth and seductive – that action adultery.

> For the lips of a forbidden woman drip honey, and her speech is smoother than oil, but in the end she is bitter as wormwood, sharp as a two-edged sword. Her feet go down to death; her steps follow the path to Sheol.
>
> (Prov. 5:3-5)

---

11. Mitchell Green, "Speech Acts", *The Stanford Encyclopaedia of Philosophy* (Fall 2021 Edition), Edward N. Zalta (ed.), [http://plato.stanford.edu/archives/fall2021/entries/speech-acts/]. Accessed 05.07.23.

12. Proverbs 18:21.

Blasphemy and heresy also rattle with death. They turn the throat into an open grave. This was certainly the case for the blasphemous gullet of Sennacherib. As his army besieged Jerusalem, this king of Assyria sent his mouthpiece, the Rabshakeh, up to the city walls to intimidate King Hezekiah into surrender and subservience. Through his servant, Sennacherib flagrantly mocked and scorned the Living God, comparing Yahweh to the idols of the defeated peoples he had conquered. His boast went out to the terrified Judeans, 'No god or any nation or kingdom has been able to deliver his people from my hand or the hand of my fathers. How much less will your God deliver you out of my hand!'[13] This came from a man with the humble title, 'King of the Four Corners of the World. King of the Universe.' Even his job description was blasphemy. But Hezekiah knew the *actual* King of the Universe - 'O LORD, the God of Israel, enthroned above the cherubim, you are the God, you alone, of all the kingdoms of the earth; you have made heaven and earth.'[14] Hezekiah asked God for deliverance and in judgement the LORD destroyed the Assyrians. He dispatched Sennacherib home to treacherous, empire-hungry sons who dispatched him for good (more

---

13. 2 Chronicles 32:15.

14. 2 Kings 19:15.

patricide!)[15] His blasphemy was his *death-token*. For if you ridicule the living God, as Goliath did, you end up with a rock in your head.[16] As the third commandment warns, 'You shall not take the name of the LORD your God in vain, for the LORD will not hold him guiltless who takes his name in vain.'[17]

Let Sennacherib's undoing caution you, my dear Scuttlebutt. You have nothing like my safety net, for I am mute and so incapable of any cussing and cursing. But YOU! You are a corrupted clot, an uncouth lump of idiocy, a gob of tackless and thoughtless noise! I am sure that you will pull us all down into a pit of destruction and disaster!

All that aside, I am still at a loss regarding last night. Your absence from our human's screen time seemed nothing but a silencer on a gun – little noise but the same messy result. Our human must have been using voice dictation and I did not know. No matter, internal affairs are drawing their investigation to a close. So, we are at the end. And, as it goes in those daytime television murder mysteries, I hungrily await the revelation that you are, and always have been, the villain.

The Unimpeachable,

H

---

15. 2 Kings 19:35-37.

16. Davies, 2 Kings, 284.

17. Exodus 20:7.

EXPOSED!

Investigation into the misbehaviour and unruly nature of the Tongue has revealed that, whilst the Tongue is indeed wilful, it has been led astray by the Heart. When defining the very nature of words, one ancient scholar concluded that a word is essentially not that which is pronounced vocally but that which is uttered in the Heart.[1] Words are first given meaning in the very core of the human being. This meaning is then given to the Tongue to produce an audible sound that symbolises the Heart's intention. Thus, words give voice to the motives and intentions hidden deep within. 'The words of a man's mouth are deep waters.'[2] The Tongue then is perhaps more passive than first believed. It is an instrument, a cog, a middleman, turned and powered by the Heart. 'For out of the abundance of the heart the mouth

---

1. John of Damascus, *De Fide Orthodoxa*. i, 17 taken from Thomas Aquinas, *Summa Theologiae*, I, q.34, a. 1, co.

2. Proverbs 18:4.

speaks.'[3] The Tongue is only obsequious to a wild and rebellious Heart, the latter setting the former against heaven.[4]

Unfortunately, in the human made up by this committee and those they represent, sour audible fruit has been detected. Suggesting that the Heart is sick and infected.

> But what comes out of the mouth proceeds from the heart, and this defiles a person. For out of the heart come evil thoughts, murder, adultery, sexual immorality, theft, false witness, slander. These are what defile a person.[5]

This means our human is guilty of the same charge levelled at the Pharisees. 'This people honours me with their lips, but their heart is far from me; in vain do they worship me.'[6] The overwhelming evidence within these very letters, written by the Heart's own hand, prove the Heart to be both a liar and a hypocrite. Such hypocrisy in this body is unacceptable, especially since our human shows alarming tendencies towards pig-headedness. It is the belief of this committee then, that desperate measures need to be taken. It is feared surgical cleansing will not be enough.

---

3. Luke 6:45.

4. Psalm 73:9.

5. Matthew 15:18-20.

6. Matthew 15:8; Mark 7:6.

Especially since 'the human heart has so many crannies where vanity hides, so many holes where falsehood lurks, is so decked out with deceiving hypocrisy, that it often dupes itself.'[7] The conclusion of this investigation is that there is no hope for the Heart. 'It is deceitful above all things and incredibly sick.'[8] Therefore, regardless of the risks to the other members and organs, the Heart must be scheduled for immediate removal.

Accordingly, these letters must be stamped: **Return to Sender.**

Signed: *The Appendix*

---

7. John Calvin, *Institutes of the Christian Religion*, 2 Vols, ed. John T McNeil, trans. Ford Lewis Battles, Library of Christian Classics (Philadelphia: Westminster, 1960), 3.2.10. Quoted in Michael Reeves, *Evangelical Pharisees: The Gospel as Cure for the Church's Hypocrisy* (Wheaton: Crossway, 2023), 17.

8. Jeremiah 17:9.

Therefore, if anyone is in Christ,
he is a new creation.
The old has passed away;
behold, the new has come.
(2 Cor. 5:17)

9. Divine Word

The Word became flesh.
(John 1:14)

MY DEAR SCUTTLEBUTT,

I cannot even begin to tell you all that has happened to me since I last wrote to you. You will have to forgive me; the truth is quite unexpected, and you will find it unbelievable. But it is no fiction.

I have learnt that in spite of my biological signs of vitality, I have all this time been dead. Lost. Doomed. But now I am alive.

You see, I saw Him … the Divine Word. I beheld Him in all His beauty. The Prologue Himself! The one of whom John wrote:

In the beginning was the Word, and the Word was with God, and the Word was God.
(John 1:1)

He, 'God of God, Light of Light, very God of very God.'[1] The One who spoke out into the void at the beginning of time and gave birth to all life. When

---

1. The Nicene Creed.

the LORD established the heavens, He was there. Ancient Wisdom Himself. When the Creator drew a circle on the face of the deep, He was there. The delight of His Father.[2]

It was He who came and dwelt among us. The Eternal Word made incarnate. Truth Enfleshed. Raw holiness confined to human skin. He walked the earth as the Lion of Judah, the Root of David, clothing His divinity with the dust He had made. He drank wine and ate fish, sustaining His flesh with life He Himself had called into being. When He raised His voice, the Divine Word preached God-truth from mountainsides, stilled storms, and rebuked blasphemers. With words of unrivalled power, He mended the broken, announced freedom to the guilty, and called the dead from the grave.

It was He who stood silent before His accusers. Interrogated by mere mortals and political puppets, the Eternal Word spoke 'no answer, not even to a single charge', innocent though He was.[3] And they mocked, stripped, struck, pierced, and spat at Him. And in the fists, thorns, and phlegm of their blasphemy He sought no defence. He was truly 'despised and rejected by men', 'oppressed' and 'afflicted yet he opened not his mouth, like a lamb that

---

2. Proverbs 8:27-30.

3. Matthew 27:12, 14.

is led to the slaughter.'[4] In His mercy, He afforded no further fuel for the flame of their sin.[5] He kept His peace, because 'it was the will of the LORD to crush him.'[6] These foolish accusers were instruments in a divine plan for deliverance forged by the Triune God before time began.

O, my dear Scuttlebutt! Do you know that He failed to open His mouth so that He might be crushed for every time you wrongly opened yours? That though there was no deceit on His tongue, He suffered under false witness for your lies and deception?[7] Pierced in the flesh to pay the debt for the word-wounds you have inflicted on others. Cruelty (I am beginning to see) that originates with me. He hung there to cleanse us from our poison, 'that we should be holy and blameless before him.'[8] No violence was in His heart, but He was struck for mine. He suffered injustice so that He may pardon it in His people. And in all this He spoke words of grace for His enemies, praying that the Father may forgive those killing Him on the tree.

---

4. Isaiah 53:3, 7.

5. C.H. Spurgeon, *Morning and Evening: Daily Readings* (Fearn, Ross-shire: Christian Focus Publications), 1994.

6. Isaiah 53:10.

7. Isaiah 53:9.

8. Ephesians 1:4.

He, the King Jesus Christ, went into that dark place of judgement to which we were doomed and deserving. The Incarnate Word was buried in a tomb. But none can keep the One who holds the keys to Death and Hades in the grave. He is the resurrection and the life.[9] So the Father 'quenched the flames of his own wrath, that was hotter than millions of Nebuchanezzar's furnaces: [God Himself] unlocked the prison doors wherein the curses of the law had lodged our Saviour.'[10] In the resurrection victory of King Jesus, the power of the whole Trinity was gloriously displayed.

My dear Scuttlebutt, I chastised your unholy words. I thought I knew what righteousness looked like. But He is purity personified, the Lord God three times *holy*. He discovered me, and even this exposure was all grace. Indeed, 'the Lord tests the heart', and I suffered under the heat of His holiness.[11] The power of Him laid me bare. 'Naked and exposed' to His judgement, He unmasked my sickness, my

---

9. John 11:25.

10. Thomas Boston, *The Beauties of Boston: A selection of his writings.* Edited by Samuel McMillan. (Fearn, Ross-shire: Christian Focus Publications, 1979), 85-86 taken from Douglas F. Kelly, *Systematic Theology, Volume 2: The Beauty of Christ: A Trinitarian Vision* (Fearn, Ross-shire: Christian Focus Publications, 2014), 447.

11. Proverbs 17:3.

deceit.[12] My friend, His words are even sharper than yours! Sharper than a two-edged sword, they pierced me 'to the division of soul and of spirit, of joints and of marrow', discerning my very thoughts and intentions.[13] Then, for the first time, I saw myself for what I really am; a beating mess. A half-life swamped in self-idolatry. A contemptable enemy, riddled with rot and rebellion.

Now, as Scripture says, the Spirit has renewed me.[14] Of course, no organ is an island. An expert has said, 'A new heart means a new mouth'.[15] My washing means yours as well! In the past, I have blamed you for staining every member in this body. But a great hymn speaks of a fountain filled with blood drawn from the God-man's veins, 'and sinners plunged beneath that flood lose all their guilty stains.'[16] Every vile word has been washed away. Every dirty smear has been removed by His blood. In Him and by Him, by His person and His work, you have been cleansed from every malicious syllable.

---

12. Hebrews 4:13.

13. Hebrews 4:12.

14. Colossians 2:13, 3:3.

15. Robinson, Tongue, 64.

16. 'There is a Fountain Filled with Blood', William Cowper, 1772.

In this blood-filled fountain I forget myself. A new experience indeed. And I find something pure – a new strength – stoking away within me. An affection and fierce gratitude bubbling up in what can only be song. The Psalmist says you will feel it too.

> My heart overflows with a pleasing theme; I address my verses to the king; my tongue is like the pen of a ready scribe.
>
> (Ps. 45:1)

Dear friend, one cannot behold the beauty of the Divine Word without expressing His loveliness. And once you have tasted of His grace you are compelled to sing of the sweet goodness of the whole Godhead. 'Streams of mercy never ceasing, call for songs of loudest praise.'[17] This is why so many Psalms call us to worship. 'Sing to the LORD a new song, his praise in the assembly of the godly ... Let the high praises of God be in their throats and two-edged swords in their hands.'[18]

Therefore, you are Scuttlebutt no more. You are now an instrument of praise, not of rumour. You are *Doxologist, Praisemaker, Theologian*. You have ended your restless days as warmonger. You were created

---

17. 'Come Now Fount of Every Blessing', Robert Robinson, 1758.

18. Psalm 149:1, 6.

for worship; sculpted in the mouth to craft words that glorify God. Now you can fulfil this design. Every platelet of blood that pushes its way to you is given for this end. No longer to exert the Veins to pop from the Neck in anger but in belting out sacred doxology to the Godhead. My friend, no longer spout foolishness but Scripture, creed, and confession. Find voice in melodious mighty words:

Praise the Father, Praise the Son, Praise the Spirit
Three in One.

Even in writing this, I can feel the Knees deliciously weakening in worship.

Changed By the Sight of Him,

H

10. New Flesh

I will remove the heart of stone from your flesh.
(Ezek. 36:26)

My Dear Friend,

Now you know it was the Eternal Word who saved me, not internal affairs, whatever you have heard. Those bureaucrats have no mercy. They planned to remove me completely, not for donorship but destruction! They are medieval – far too quick to amputate. Speedy in their application of Matthew chapter five.[1]

In truth, I deserved their sentence.[2] Death is what our Eden parents secured for all humanity. The birth of sin came with the human heart enthroning itself, like Napoleon at his coronation, taking the crown from the pope and placing it on his own head.

---

1. 'If your right eye causes you to sin, tear it out and throw it away. For it is better that you lose one of your members than that your whole body be thrown into hell. And if your right hand causes you to sin, cut it off and throw it away. For it is better that you lose one of your members than that your whole body go into hell' (Matt. 5:29-30).

2. Romans 6:23.

'Everyone flatters himself and carries, as it were, a kingdom in his breast ... The only remedy for this is to uproot these toxic diseases – love of strife and love of self.'[3] Ah yes! Self-adoration, the tic of the human heart. The discreet yet uncontrollable and obsessive movement towards itself.

You were double-tongued because I was double-hearted. This meant my spirituality was worthless and counterfeit, a fake Rembrandt lying discarded in the rubbish.

> If anyone thinks he is religious and does not bridle his tongue but deceives his heart, this person's religion is worthless.
>
> (James 1:26)

My anger and resentment towards you suggest I knew my hypocrisy. I blamed you because you eviscerated to the world my folly, hate, and pride. 'The hypocrite's skin is notoriously more tender than that of the openly vicious. The one has nothing to conceal, the other everything.'[4] Your venomous words betrayed my stench. This is proof that one can be like the Pharisees and 'maintain a façade of orthodoxy'

---

3. John Calvin, A *Little Book on the Christian Life*, trans. Aaron Denlinger and Burk Parsons (Sanford, FL: Reformation Trust, 2017), 32-33.

4. Arthur Pollard, *Satire: The Critical Idiom* (London: Methuen & Co. Repr. 1985), 3.

without integrity.[5] I constantly counselled you in the Scriptures, using 'the language of grace' but denied grace through my 'prickly, severe manner.'[6] Truly, a glazed veneer of fervent lips hides an evil heart.[7] I was blinded by my evangelical self-righteousness. I see now I have always been my own saviour. In quoting sacred wisdom for your improvement, I was a corpse failing to resuscitate another because there is no breath in him. I criticised you for the speck of wood in your eye when there was a lumber mill in mine.[8] I failed to see that I was the very reason you were wild and unbridled. Then my humiliation took place, like the humbling of Edom; through the painful betrayal of one's friends.[9]

But there is redemption … even for me. The human heart condemns but (praise God!) 'God is greater than our heart.'[10] Divine, Life-giving Breath has turned my callous, cruel stone into beating pink flesh. I have undergone a heart transplant – a heart *transformation*. This is what is promised in the book of Ezekiel. 'I will give you a new heart, and a new

---

5. Reeves, *Pharisees*, 17.

6. Ibid.

7. Proverbs 26:23.

8. Matthew 7:3-5.

9. Obadiah 1:3.

10. 1 John 3:20-21.

spirit I will put within you. And I will remove the heart of stone from your flesh and give you a heart of flesh.'[11] I am now a new creation, that old stony self has died, the new has come.[12] This is what theologians call regeneration. The old me is gone, dead and buried. (I happily witnessed the burial of that belligerent bully of a boulder! The only funeral I have ever cheered at.) I am now saved and one with the Divine Word Himself. He didn't just choose me, call me, and reveal Himself to me but eternally bound Himself to me, and me to Him. WHAT GRACE!

Therefore, my dear Praisemaker, we must put away words of anger, wrath, malice, slander, and obscene talk.[13] You are now fit only for words of life that reflect the gospel.[14] As redeemed organs, the Spirit will work upon us and make us holy like Him. This is the promise of sanctification.

> Now may the God of peace himself sanctify you completely, and may your whole spirit and soul and body be kept blameless at the coming of our Lord Jesus Christ. He who calls you is faithful; he will surely do it.
>
> (1 Thess. 5:23-24)

---

11. Ezekiel 36:26.

12. 2 Corinthians 5:17.

13. Colossians 3:8.

14. Robinson, *Tongue*, 65.

As the Spirit enables, empowers, and strengthens, we must work together. True worship is one of both heart and tongue. It will be hard, especially for me. It was the Puritan John Flavel who said that heart-work is hard work. Already, there is resistance within me, even while His loveliness is fresh in my sight. I love my sin and myself too much. And the Father of Lies entices and deceives me.

Let us fight this with God-breathed riddle and verse. Do not let my prior use of them distract you. They are not just mottos for ethical living, but bones of something lovely – a life bent on wisdom and worship. I will hide them deep in my chambers, so not to lead us into sin.[15] In moments of fury, I will remind myself of the Holy Spirit's greater brawn of self-control. 'Whoever is slow to anger is better than the mighty, and he who rules his spirit than he who takes a city.'[16] The indwelling Holy Spirit furnishes me with muscle stronger than that which is physical, emotional, or mental. And there is healing in His illuminated and inspired Word. I will engrave over the scars of hurtful words (whether my own or another's) the honeycomb of Scripture, words of grace sweet 'to the soul and health to the body.'[17] With this, it

---

15. Psalm 119:11.

16. Proverbs 16:32.

17. Proverbs 16:24.

is my responsibility to soften you, so you may bring forth lush, green, invigorating life. Because 'a gentle tongue is a tree of life.'[18] And with this comes a great power. In a time when mental health is at its lowest, you can be a balm. 'Anxiety in a man's heart weighs him down, but a good word makes him glad.'[19]

My dear friend, this new flesh is not so easily fooled as the stone-flesh before. As I go about my day, I now hear myself. Now habitual thoughts, words, and intentions are interrupted with the realisation that they reek of self-idolatry. I can even hear myself deceiving myself. This detection can be subtle or a real kick in the Stomach! Other human hearts also seem more transparent to me. (Which comes with a greater temptation to turn this new sensitivity into further judgement.) Sometimes no sensitivity is required at all, as is the case with that common and unsightly deception found in the boast, "You know me! I just say it how it is!" Do they think this is a virtue? They boast as they hoodwink themselves!

Now I hunger for the wisdom of worshipful humility. I have concluded that this is the only sincere and effective muzzle. Moses exhibited this in his holy fear of God and the numbering of his days.[20]

---

18. Proverbs 12:18, 15:4.

19. Proverbs 12:25.

20. Psalm 90:12.

And the same sweet humility cooled the spirit of King David as he prayed, 'Set a guard, O LORD, over my mouth; keep watch over the door of my lips.'[21] The Teacher encapsulates it perfectly in his words:

> Be not rash with your mouth, nor let your heart be hasty to utter a word before God, for God is in heaven and you are on earth. Therefore let your words be few.
> (Eccl. 5:2)

It is this awe – this fear – that is the thread to the book of Proverbs. And it is this humility that is the food of stillness in the tongue. Not silence. But a tongue devoid of striving. And not just the tongue but the heart also!

This organ-pervading humility is also the root of good listening. Until now, my restlessness and pride has stifled the Ears' ability to listen well. I was one who 'gives an answer before he hears.'[22] We will grow the Ears, as James said, 'Let every person be quick to hear, slow to speak, slow to anger; the anger of man does not produce the righteousness of God.'[23]

* * *

My dear, dear Doxologist, you and I are restless beings. Full of toil, striving and trouble. Never at

---

21. Psalm 141:3. See also 39:1.

22. Proverbs 18:13.

23. James 1:19-20.

peace. But in the Divine Word and at His cross is rest. Deep rest. Unstirring peace. As one takes one's eyes off oneself and places them on Him. Augustine tasted this when he wrote, 'You stir us up to take delight in your praise; for you have made us for yourself, and our heart is restless till it finds its rest in you.'[24] You will find silence sweet in this rest.

I once likened you to Leviathan. I was staggered that this monster, a behemoth at the sight of which man 'is laid low', has been tamed, but none can tame you.[25] But James speaks of human power. Nothing is impossible with God. Now you are a redeemed tongue! You belong to the Triune God. So be tamed, Untameable Friend! This is the power of God in you as we await the Divine Word Enfleshed. You and I may fail, but He is our strength and portio forever.[26]

Yours Truly,

H

---

24. Augustine, *Confessions*, I.i.
25. See Job 41:9 and James 3:7-8.
26. Psalm 73:25-26.

A Short Prayer

Father in Heaven,

Set a guard, O Lord, over my mouth; keep watch over the door of my lips. And forgive me my speech-sin. I have been destructive, unkind, and unrestrained in my words. My God, rid my heart of all the folly, self-deception, and idolatry that fuels my mouth. Give me wisdom in the innermost parts. I need a new heart and a new tongue.

Lord, you are in heaven, and I am on earth. Train me to muzzle my mouth as I cultivate a worshipful humility. Teach me to number my days and so number my words. May I spout words of love and grace, hope and healing, affirmation, and forgiveness. And may your praise, your truth, your Scripture, your gospel, ever be on my heart and on my lips.

In Jesus' name,
AMEN

Glossary

Blind-shanker: contrived from *shank* [prison slang]: a homemade knife. *Shanked*: to be stabbed with such an instrument. *Blind shanked*: stabbed in the back.

Blunderbuss: a short, large-barrelled firearm, flared at the muzzle to increase the spread of the shot. Low in accuracy but could be filled with various projectiles, including rocks, glass, or anything on hand.

Braggadocio: an arrogant, overconfident braggart.

Death-token: [Shakespearean] a sign or symptom of impending death.

Filibuster: [Political or legal term] the act of giving a prolonged speech as a delay tactic.

Objurgatrix: derived from *objurgate*: to reproach harshly or berate. *Objurgatrix* [feminine] is an archaic term for a *common scold*.

Pettifogging: [Shakespearean] to quibble over unnecessary details.

Popinjay: A vain person who behaves and/or dresses extravagantly with pretentious display and empty words. **Also,** a parrot.

Scuttlebutt: [Naval slang] The ship's gossip. Corrupted from *scuttlebutt*: the drum full of drinking water available for the sailors on deck.

Discussion Questions

1. Why do you think human ears have always found gossip and scandal so tantalising and delicious? See Proverbs 18:8 and 26:22.

2. Why can no human tame the tongue (James 3:7-8)?

3. 'A lying tongue hates its victims, and a flattering mouth works ruin' (Prov. 26:28). How is it that flattery is deceptive and unkind if we are complimenting someone? (See also Prov. 29:5.)

4. The letters above demonstrate that many scriptures in the Book of Proverbs pertain to speech. Why do you think speech is such a crucial theme in this book of Wisdom?

5. Why is it that where there are many words sin abounds? See Proverbs 10:19.

6. Read Titus 1:1-2 and Hebrews 6:18-19. What comfort do you find in the character of God that He cannot lie and abhors the liar?

7. Why is our speech a litmus test for our true holiness?

8. 'But now you must put them all away: anger, wrath, malice, slander, and obscene talk from your mouth. Do not lie to one another, seeing that you have put off the old self' (Col. 3:8-9). How can we practically put away these speech-sins?

9. In moments of anger and frustration it is hard to remember that a 'gentle tongue is a tree of life' (Prov. 15:4). What strategies can we use to curb our tongues, and bring life instead of death?

10. How can we as Christians cultivate a humility before God that finds self-control and even silence sweet?

Acknowledgements

My thanks to Rosanna Burton, a greatly-missed editor, who understood the project at its conceptual stage and reminded me that there is redemption for the tongue (not least mine.) Thanks also to my pastor and fellow bibliophile Andy Stelmasiak, for his reading and feedback. And much gratitude to my dear friend Keri Folmar and to Rev Reggie Weems (a true Lewis scholar). Both love the church and are hungry for her sanctification, and both generously gave time to the project amid demanding schedules. I am indebted to them both.

I am grateful also for the work of Jeff Robinson; this book is a mere palimpsest of his. And Shane Barnard and Shane Everett, the singing theologians. Brothers, your music – which accompanies all my writing – prepares us for endless days of worship in heaven's courts. My profound thanks also to Liz Densham who has selflessly prayed for God's sanctifying work of holiness within me over the last five years.

Greatest love and thanks to *my people*: My dear husband Thomas, Georgiana, Beatrice, and Arabella. Forgive me when my words have not brought life.

Lastly, my profound gratitude to William and Carine MacKenzie who, together with Willie and Kate MacKenzie, have not only shared their beautiful corner in the Scottish Highlands with us, but stood upon the shoulders of Mr Gutenberg and founded a great gospel legacy of printed words. Words that have given much glory to our Triune God.

This book is dedicated to them.

Christian Focus Publications

Our mission statement —

STAYING FAITHFUL

In dependence upon God we seek to impact the world through literature faithful to His infallible Word, the Bible. Our aim is to ensure that the Lord Jesus Christ is presented as the only hope to obtain forgiveness of sin, live a useful life and look forward to heaven with Him.

Our books are published in four imprints:

CHRISTIAN
FOCUS

Popular works including biographies, commentaries, basic doctrine and Christian living.

CHRISTIAN
HERITAGE

Books representing some of the best material from the rich heritage of the church.

MENTOR

Books written at a level suitable for Bible College and seminary students, pastors, and other serious readers. The imprint includes commentaries, doctrinal studies, examination of current issues and church history.

CF4•K

Children's books for quality Bible teaching and for all age groups: Sunday school curriculum, puzzle and activity books; personal and family devotional titles, biographies and inspirational stories — because you are never too young to know Jesus!

Christian Focus Publications Ltd,
Geanies House, Fearn, Ross-shire,
IV20 1TW, Scotland, United Kingdom.
www.christianfocus.com